Sanatan Synergy

31 Days to a Fulfilled You

Sanatan Synergy

31 Days to a Fulfilled You

Embracing Wisdom, Prosperity, and Joy through Ancient Teachings

SHANTILAL PATEL

Qurate
quratebooks.com
Because everyone has a story to tell

Book Creation Services

by

BookMyStory®

It's time to tell your story

www.bookmystorypublishing.com

A venture of

R&S Enterprises

Sanatan Synergy
Shantilal Patel

Published in 2024

© Published by

Qurate
qauratebooks.com

Qurate Books Pvt. Ltd.
Goa 403523, India
www.quratebooks.com
Tel: 1800-210-6527, Email: info@quratebooks.com

ISBN: 978-93-58989-13-7

Contents

Dedication

To my parents, Mulji and Devkiben Patel, whose unwavering love, wisdom, and quiet sacrifices laid the very foundation upon which my life stands. Their legacy is etched in the marrow of my bones, and I carry it forward with reverence.

Kokila, my steadfast compass, my North Star—your unwavering support and gentle encouragement have been my lifeline. Your strength, like the roots of ancient trees, anchors me through life's tempests. Your kindness, a beacon that guides me home.

Darshan, Deepak Bhadani and Nidhi Bhadani, my laughter-bearers, my joy-bringers—your giggles echo through the corridors of my soul. In your eyes, I glimpse the wonder of existence, and in your dreams, I find purpose. May life's canvas be painted with hues of your happiness.

Payal, Pallavi, and Avanti, daughters by choice—your presence, like sun-kissed petals, graces my days. Your care, a soothing balm for weary hearts, and your understanding, a bridge across generations. Together, we form a tapestry of shared moments.

Shardaben and Tulsidasbhai, Vinod and Priya—my siblings, my confidantes. Through storms and sunsets, we've weathered life's tides. Our bonds, unbreakable as ancient oaths, remind me that kinship transcends bloodlines.

Sunita, Jay, Omkar, Vivek, and Jash—nephews and nieces, the sparks that light my path. Your laughter, a symphony of possibility, and your curiosity, a compass pointing toward discovery. May your journeys be as rich as the stories you carry.

Krisha, Vaidehi, and Naman—my grandchildren, the promise of tomorrow. Your hugs, like warm sunbeams, melt away the years. In your eyes, I glimpse eternity, and in your innocence, I find renewal.

To friends who became family, teachers who ignited flames within, mentors who whispered courage into my veins—I raise my pen in gratitude. You've shaped my learning journey, etching wisdom upon my heart.

This book Sanatan Synergy, inked with memories and bound by love, is my offering—a testament to resilience, to the fragile beauty of human connections. May its pages resonate with others, weaving them into this grand existence.

Preface

I am Shantilal Patel. By training, I'm an electronic engineer and a management studies graduate. In 1992, I founded an electronics manufacturing and sales company, and since then, I have been successfully running it. However, my journey is not just limited to the world of electronics and management. I have always been deeply drawn to spirituality. As a spiritual seeker, I have spent my life learning and practicing the universal laws found in Sanatan Dharma.

Sanatan Dharma, with its beautiful traditions and teachings passed down from generation to generation, is one of the oldest practices given to us by extraordinarily intuitive and universally tuned minds. So many spiritual practices around the world have their roots in Sanatan Dharma.

In today's world, it's easy for people to focus on just a few spiritual practices that resonate with them—maybe something that helps with the body, mind, emotions, or soul. But sometimes, with limited knowledge, people often start believing that this is the only path and connect it too closely with their religious beliefs. When that happens, it can be hard to see the bigger picture of Sanatan Dharma as a whole and all the learnings it has to offer.

We might even start to think of some aspects of Sanatan Dharma as just religious beliefs, which can easily hold us back from truly understanding its universal laws and experiencing the deep personal growth it encourages. Sadly, this lack of understanding often leads to suffering. Even with all our technical advancements and diverse spiritual practices, the world is suffering more than ever. And I believe it's because many of us haven't been taught the complete values and practices of Sanatan Dharma. Without that guidance, this results in increased emotional problems like greed, enmity, and prejudice, to name a few.

At present, we have many wonderful teachers sharing their spiritual practices around the world in different cultures. It's important to remember, dear reader, that all these practices and teachings are meant to empower you, to nurture and strengthen your own unique Sanatan Values. Whether you're studying a book, learning from a teacher, or listening to a religious preacher, let your intention always be to enhance, build, and align yourself with the beautiful principles of Sanatan Dharma.

This book is for everyone who is actively exploring true spiritual growth and yearning to understand the reality of life. I have included the names and authors of books that will help you learn and master the Sanatan Values. I have endeavored to make your life purpose easy to learn, understand and start the journey that is clear, fulfilling, and deeply satisfying.

This book is an invitation to journey into the very heart of Sanatan Dharma, and I hope it serves as a valuable guide for you, dear reader. Each chapter delves into a specific value, providing a detailed explanation and recommending a book for further reading. My aim is to share a comprehensive understanding of these values and how they guide our lives.

Written in simple English, this book is meant to be accessible to readers in India and all around the world.

May you find joy and enlightenment on this beautiful journey!

Shantilal Patel

Day 1

Dharma (धर्म)

Dharma, a Sanskrit term that is often translated as "duty," "religion," or "moral law," is a fundamental concept not only in Hinduism but also in Buddhism, Jainism, and Sikhism[1]. In the context of Sanatan Dharma, Dharma refers to the moral and ethical duties that one must uphold according to their station in life. It is the guiding principle that helps us make the right decisions in life[1].

Understanding Dharma

The word Dharma comes from the Sanskrit root "dhṛ" which means "to sustain" or "that which is integral to something". For example, the Dharma of sugar is to be sweet, and the Dharma of fire is to be hot. In the human context, Dharma consists of duties that sustain them according to their innate characteristics, which are both spiritual and material.

Dharma is often considered to be the very foundation of life. It is that which holds the society together. The concept of Dharma is beautifully explained in the "Bhagavad Gita", a sacred text of Hinduism.

The Role of Dharma in Daily Life

Dharma plays a crucial role in guiding our actions in daily life. It serves as a moral compass, guiding us to make decisions that are righteous and beneficial not only for ourselves but also for the society at large. Upholding Dharma leads to harmony and peace in society, while neglecting Dharma can lead to conflict and suffering[1].

Practical Application of Dharma

To apply the concept of Dharma in our daily lives, we need to understand our responsibilities and duties in the various roles we play. As students, our Dharma might be to study diligently and respect our teachers. As parents, our Dharma might be to nurture and guide our children. As a citizen, our Dharma might be to abide by the law and contribute to the welfare of the society.

Further Reading

To delve deeper into the concept of Dharma, here are some recommended books:

1. "Dharma: Decoding the Epics for a Meaningful Life" by Amish and Bhavna Roy.
2. "The Essence of Enlightenment" by James Swartz.
3. "Bringing Home the Dharma: Awakening Right Where You Are" by Jack Kornfield.

These books provide a comprehensive understanding of Dharma and its application in daily life. They offer practical advice on how to live in accordance with Dharma and achieve peace and fulfilment.

In conclusion, as a core value of Sanatan Dharma, Dharma provides a framework for living a righteous and fulfilling life. By understanding and applying Dharma in our daily lives, we can contribute to the well-being of ourselves and society at large.

Note:

....
....
....
....
....
....

....
....
....
....
....
....

....
....

Day 2

Karma (कर्म)

Karma, a Sanskrit word meaning "action" or "deed," is a fundamental concept in Sanatan Dharma. It refers to the law of cause and effect. Every action we take, every word we speak, and every thought we hold creates an impression or a ripple of energy, leaving a lasting imprint on our soul. These impressions, or karmic imprints, accumulate over time and influence our future experiences and circumstances.

Understanding Karma

Karma is not just limited to our actions in this lifetime, but it is also believed to carry over from our past lives. In Sanatan Dharma, it is believed that we are all born with a karmic debt from our past lives, one that we must repay in this lifetime. The concept of karma helps us understand that we are the creators of our own destiny. It is through our actions we create our future, and we have the power to change our destiny by changing our actions.

The Role of Karma in Daily Life

Karma plays an important role in guiding our actions in daily life. It serves as a moral compass, encouraging us to make decisions that are righteous and beneficial not only for ourselves but also for the society at large. Upholding Karma leads to harmony and peace in society, while neglecting Karma can lead to conflict and suffering.

Practical Application of Karma

To apply the concept of Karma in our daily lives, we need to be mindful of the consequences of our actions. As students, our Karma might be to study diligently and respect our teachers. As parents, our Karma might be to nurture and guide our children with love and righteousness. As citizens, our Karma might be to abide by the law and contribute to the welfare of society.

Further Reading

If you're curious to explore Karma more deeply, here are some books I recommended:

1. "Karma: A Yogi's Guide to Crafting Your Destiny" by Sadhguru
2. "The Essence of Enlightenment" by James Swartz "Bringing Home the Dharma: Awakening Right Where You Are" by Jack Kornfield.

These books provide a comprehensive understanding of Karma and its application in our daily lives. They offer practical advice on how to live in accordance with Karma while finding peace and fulfillment along the way.

In essence, Karma, as a core value of Sanatan Dharma, provides a framework for living a life filled with righteousness and purposc. By understanding and applying Karma in our everyday lives, we can contribute to the well-being of ourselves and also for society at large.

Note:

....
....
....
....
....
....

....
....
....
....
....
....

....
....

Day 3

Ahimsa (अहिंसा)

Ahimsa, a Sanskrit word meaning non-violence, is a fundamental principle in Sanatan Dharma. It advocates compassion and respect for all living beings. Ahimsa is not just about abstaining from physical violence, but it also encompasses non-violence in our thoughts, speech, and actions.

Understanding Ahimsa

Ahimsa teaches us to treat others with the same kindness we would like to be treated. It encourages us to understand the interconnectedness of all beings and live in harmony with them. Ahimsa is beautifully encapsulated in the phrase "Praniyon Me Sadhbhavana Ho," which means having goodwill towards all living beings.

The Role of Ahimsa in Daily Life

In our daily lives, we can practice Ahimsa by being mindful of our actions and their impact on others. It encourages us to choose words that are kind and thoughtful, to act in ways that do not harm others, and to cultivate thoughts that are positive and uplifting.

Practical Application of Ahimsa

Practicing Ahimsa involves making conscious choices in our everyday lives. This could mean choosing not to harm others with our words, refraining from harmful actions, and even choosing a diet that does not cause harm to animals. "Ahimsa: The Vegan Way of Life" by Nikhil Goyal explores this concept beautifully in the context of veganism.

Further Reading

If you're longing to delve deeper into the concept of Ahimsa, here are some books I recommend:

1. "Ahimsa: Its theory and practice in Gandhism" by Dr. Ram Ponnu.
2. "The Miracle of Mindfulness" by Thich Nhat Hanh.
3. "The Power of Now" by Eckhart Tolle.

These books provide a comprehensive understanding of Ahimsa and its application in our daily lives. They offer practical advice on how to live in accordance with Ahimsa, finding peace and fulfillment along the way.

In essence, Ahimsa, a core value of Sanatan Dharma, provides a framework for living a peaceful and harmonious life. By embracing and applying Ahimsa in our everyday lives, we can contribute not only to our own well-being but also to the well-being of the entire world.

Note:

Day 4

Satya (सत्य)

Satya, often translated as "truth," is another fundamental concept in Sanatan Dharma. It refers to the practice of truthfulness and sincerity in all aspects of our live. Satya encourages us to be honest with ourselves and others. It is one of the four pillars of Dharma in the Satya Yuga, along with austerity, cleanliness, and mercy.

Understanding Satya

Satya is not just about speaking the truth, but it is also about living the truth. It is about being true to our nature and our Dharma. It's about walking a path where our thoughts, words, and actions are in alignment with what is real and truth.

The Role of Satya in Daily Life

Satya plays a crucial role in our daily lives. It serves as a moral compass, guiding us to make decisions that are righteous and beneficial. Upholding Satya leads to harmony and peace in society, while neglecting Satya can lead to conflict and suffering.

Practical Application of Satya

To apply the concept of Satya in our daily lives, we simply need to bc honest and sincere in everything we do, especially our interactions with others. This means we must speak the truth, even when it feels difficult. We must also be true to ourselves by acknowledging our strengths and weaknesses.

Further Reading

If you want to delve deeper into the concept of Satya, here are some books I recommend:

1. "Satyarth Prakash" by Swami Dayananda Saraswati.
2. "Hit Refresh: A Memoir by Microsoft's CEO" by Satya Nadella.
3. "Banaras Talkies" by Satya Vyas.

These books provide a comprehensive understanding of Satya and its application in our daily lives. They offer practical advice on how to live in alignment with Satya, finding peace and fulfillment.

In essence, Satya, as a core value of Sanatan Dharma, provides a framework for a life of integrity and purpose. By understanding and applying Satya in our everyday lives, we can contribute to the well-being of ourselves and society at large.

Note:

....
....
....
....
....
....

....
....
....
....
....
....

....
....

Day 5

Asteya (अस्तेय)

Asteya, a Sanskrit word meaning "non-stealing," is a fundamental principle in Sanatan Dharma. It calls for us to honor the sacredness of others' rights and possessions. When we embrace Asteya, we cultivate a garden of trust and mutual regard, where the fragrance of respect enriches our social bonds.

Understanding Asteya

Asteya isn't merely about refraining from physically taking something that belongs to someone else. It's about not desiring what others have, not clinging to unnecessary possessions, and not exploiting others. It's about finding contentment with what we have and respecting the belongings of others.

The Role of Asteya in Daily Life

Asteya plays a crucial role in our everyday choices. It serves as a moral compass, guiding us to make decisions that are righteous and beneficial for ourselves and society. When we uphold Asteya, it leads to harmony and peace in society, while neglecting Asteya can lead to conflict and suffering.

Practical Application of Asteya

To apply the concept of Asteya in our daily lives, we need to be mindful of the impact of our actions. If we're students, our Asteya might be to respect the intellectual property of others and not plagiarize. As professionals, our Asteya might be to respect the time and effort of our colleagues and not take credit for their work. As citizens, our Asteya might be to respect public property and not vandalize them.

Further Reading

If you want to delve deeper into the concept of Asteya, here are some books I recommend:

1. "The Yamas & Niyamas: Exploring Yoga's Ethical Practice" by Deborah Adele.
2. "Light on Yoga" by B.K.S. Iyengar.
3. "The Art of Happiness" by Dalai Lama and Howard Cutler.

These books provide a comprehensive understanding of Asteya and how we can weave it into our lives. They offer practical advice on how to live in accordance with Asteya and achieve peace and contentment along the way.

In essence, Asteya, as a core value of Sanatan Dharma, provides a framework for a life filled with righteousness and fulfillment. By understanding and applying Asteya in our everyday lives, we can contribute to the well-being not only for ourselves, but for the entire world.

Note:

....
....
....
....
....
....

....
....
....
....
....
....

....
....

Day 6

Brahmacharya (ब्रह्मचर्य)

Brahmacharya, a Sanskrit word meaning "conduct towards the realization of Brahman," is a fundamental principle in Sanatan Dharma. It is sometimes associated with celibacy or chastity, but its meaning is far deeper and broader. Brahmacharya is about practicing moderation and self-restraint in all areas of our lives. It encourages us to live a balanced life.

Understanding Brahmacharya

Brahmacharya is the first stage of one's life where one leads a life of celibacy – one that is dedicated to studies and acquisition of knowledge and skills. The word Brahmacharya itself means 'one whose activity facilitates going after the knowledge of Brahman.' In Sanskrit, 'chara' means 'engaging' or 'going after'. So the first stage of an individual's life – the first 25 years – should be spent as a Brahmachari (one who lives a life of Brahmacharya) in which one is constantly engaged in learning and acquiring knowledge.

The Role of Brahmacharya in Daily Life

Brahmacharya plays an important role in our daily lives. It serves as a moral compass, guiding us to make decisions that are good for us and for the world around us. When we honor Brahmacharya, it leads to harmony and peace in society, while neglecting Brahmacharya can lead to conflict and suffering.

Practical Application of Brahmacharya

To apply the concept of Brahmacharya in our daily lives, we need to understand the consequences of our actions. As students, our Brahmacharya might be to study diligently and respect our teachers. As professionals, our Brahmacharya might be to respect the time and effort of our colleagues and not take credit for their work. As citizens, our Brahmacharya might be to respect the public property and not vandalize it.

Further Reading

If you're curious to explore the concept of Brahmacharya, here are some books I recommend:

1. "Practice of Brahmacharya" by Swami Sivananda
2. "Twelve Pointers for Maintaining Brahmacharya" by Original Yoga
3. "Brahmacharya: Celibacy with Right Understanding" by Swami Sivananda

These books provide a comprehensive understanding of Brahmacharya and its application in daily life. They offer practical advice on how to live in accordance with Brahmacharya and achieve peace and fulfillment.

In essence, Brahmacharya, a core value of Sanatan Dharma, provides a framework for living a righteous and fulfilling life. By understanding and applying Brahmacharya in our daily lives, we create well-being not only for ourselves, but for society at large.

Note:

....
....
....
....
....
....

....
....
....
....
....
....

....
....

Day 7

Aparigraha (अपरिग्रह)

Aparigraha, a Sanskrit word meaning "non-possessiveness" or "non-greediness," is a fundamental principle in Sanatan Dharma. It refers to the practice of non-accumulation and non-attachment. Aparigraha encourages us to take only what is necessary and no more. It teaches us to find contentment in living a simple life.

Understanding Aparigraha

Aparigraha isn't merely about refraining from physically taking something that belongs to someone else. It is also about not coveting what others have, not hoarding unnecessary possessions, and not taking advantage of other. It is about being content with what we have and respecting the belongings of others.

The Role of Aparigraha in Daily Life

Aparigraha plays a quiet yet essential role in guiding our choices each day. It's like a moral compass, guiding us to make decisions that are fair and kind not only for ourselves but also for society at large. Upholding Aparigraha leads to harmony and peace in society, while neglecting Aparigraha can lead to conflict and suffering.

Practical Application of Aparigraha

To apply the concept of Aparigraha in our daily lives, we simply need to be mindful of the impact of our actions. As students, our Aparigraha might be to respect the intellectual property of others and not plagiarize. As professionals, our Aparigraha might be to respect the time and effort of our colleagues and not take credit for their work. And as citizens, our Aparigraha might be to respect public spaces and not vandalize them.

Further Reading

If you want to delve deeper into the concept of Aparigraha, here are some books I recommend:

1. "The Yamas & Niyamas: Exploring Yoga's Ethical Practice" by Deborah Adele.
2. "Light on Yoga" by B.K.S. Iyengar.
3. "The Art of Simple Living" by Shunmyo Masuno.

These books provide a comprehensive understanding of Aparigraha and its application in daily life. They offer practical advice on how to live in accordance with Aparigraha and achieve peace and fulfillment.

In essence, Aparigraha, as a core value of Sanatan Dharma, provides a framework for a life filled with contentment and generosity. By embracing and applying Aparigraha in our daily lives, we can contribute to the well-being of ourselves and society at large.

Note:

....
....
....
....
....
....

....
....
....
....
....
....

....
....
....
....

Day 8

Santosha (संतोष)

Santosha, a Sanskrit word meaning "contentment," is a fundamental principle in Sanatan Dharma. It speaks to the practice of finding joy and gratitude in the present moment. Santosha encourages us to be happy and content with what we have.

Understanding Santosha

Santosha is not merely about refraining from wanting more than what we have. It's a deeper invitation to finding contentment and gratitude in our present circumstances. It is about embracing what we have and finding joy in the simple blessings of life.

The Role of Santosha in Daily Life

Santosha, dear reader, plays a crucial role in our daily lives. It serves as a moral compass, guiding us to make decisions that are righteous and beneficial not only for ourselves but also for the society at large. When we nurture Santosha, our hearts open to peace and contentment, not just for ourselves, but for the world around us, but neglecting Santosha can lead to feelings of dissatisfaction and unrest.

Practical Application of Santosha

To apply the concept of Santosha in our daily lives, we need to understand the consequences of our actions. As students, our Santosha might be to study diligently and respect our teachers. As professionals, our Santosha might be to respect the time and effort of our colleagues and not take credit for their work. As citizens, our Santosha might be to respect the public property and not vandalize it.

Further Reading

To delve deeper into the concept of Santosha, here are some recommended books:

1. "The Yamas & Niyamas: Exploring Yoga's Ethical Practice" by Deborah Adele.
2. "Light on Yoga" by B.K.S. Iyengar.
3. "The Power of Now" by Eckhart Tolle.

These books provide a comprehensive understanding of Santosha and how we can apply it in our daily lives. They offer practical advice on how to live in accordance with Santosha and find peace and fulfillment along the journey.

In essence, Santosha, as a core value of Sanatan Dharma, provides a framework for living a righteous and fulfilling life. By understanding and applying Santosha in our daily lives, we can contribute to the well-being of ourselves and society at large.

Note:

....
....
....
....
....
....

....
....
....
....
....
....

....
....
....
....

Day 9

Tapas (तपस्)

Tapas, a Sanskrit word meaning "heat" or "austerity," is a fundamental principle in Sanatan Dharma. It refers to the practice of self-discipline and austerity to attain spiritual growth. Tapas encourages the practice of self-discipline and focus in our spiritual practices.

Understanding Tapas

The word Tapas comes from the Sanskrit root "tap," which means "to heat, to give out warmth, to shine, to burn." The term evolves also to mean "to suffer, to mortify the body, undergo penance" in order to "burn away past karma" and liberate oneself. Ultimately, Tapas signifies "warmth, heat, fire" within us.

The Role of Tapas in Daily Life

Tapas plays a crucial role in our daily lives. It is like a spark of determination, encouraging us to make decisions that are aligned with righteousness and beneficial not only for ourselves but also for society. Embracing Tapas leads to harmony and peace in society, while neglecting Tapas can lead to conflict and suffering.

Practical Application of Tapas

Tapas, a beautiful concept in our everyday life, simply means being mindful of how our actions affect those around us. As students, our Tapas might be to study diligently and respect our teachers. As professionals, our Tapas might be to respect the time and effort of our colleagues and not take credit for their work. As citizens, our Tapas is about treating public spaces with kindness.

Further Reading

If you'd like to learn more about the concept of Tapas, here are some books I recommend:

1. "The Yamas & Niyamas: Exploring Yoga's Ethical Practice" by Deborah Adele.
2. "Light on Yoga" by B.K.S. Iyengar.
3. "Tapas: A Guide to Balanced Living" by Arvind Devalia.

These books provide a comprehensive understanding of Tapas and its application in daily life. They offer practical advice on how to live in accordance with Tapas and achieve peace and fulfillment.

In essence, Tapas, as a core value of Sanatan Dharma, provides a framework for living a righteous and fulfilling life. By understanding and applying Tapas in our daily life, we're not just making ourselves happier, but also making the world a better place.

Note:

....
....
....
....
....
....

....
....
....
....
....
....

....
....

Day 10

Moksha (मोक्ष)

Moksha, a Sanskrit word that translates to "liberation," is the ultimate goal of life in Sanatan Dharma. It refers to the liberation from the cycle of birth and death. Moksha is about transcending the limitations of physical existence and realizing one's true nature. It is not about escapism but about truly understanding the deeper aspects of life and existence.

Understanding Moksha

Moksha in Sanatan Dharma is closely tied to living ethically, engaging fully in life, and self-realization. It is not about leaving the world behind but about transcending the limitations of ego and material attachment while actively participating in the world with a sense of higher purpose and understanding.

The Role of Moksha in Daily Life

Moksha plays a crucial role in our daily lives. It serves as a moral compass, guiding us to make decisions that are righteous and beneficial not only for ourselves but also for the society at large. Upholding Moksha leads to harmony and peace in society, while neglecting Moksha can lead to conflict and suffering.

Practical Application of Moksha

To apply the concept of Moksha in our daily lives, we need to understand the consequences of our actions. As students, our Moksha might be to study diligently and respect our teachers. As professionals, our Moksha might be to respect the time and effort of our colleagues and not take credit for their work. As citizens, our Moksha might be to respect the public property and not vandalize it.

Further Reading

If you're curious to explore Moksha more deeply, I'd recommend these books:

1. "The Pursuit of Moksha: A Guide to Developing Awareness, Self-Realization, and Liberation" by Kameron Mackey.
2. "Freedom in Exile" by Dalai Lama.

These books provide a comprehensive understanding of Moksha and practical ways to integrate it into your daily life. They're filled with wisdom and guidance on how to live in alignment with Moksha, leading to a life filled with peace and fulfillment.

In essence, Moksha, as a core value of Sanatan Dharma, provides a framework for living a righteous and fulfilling life. By understanding and applying Moksha in our daily lives, we not only enrich our lives but also uplift the lives of others.

Note:

Day 11

Seva (सेवा)

Seva, a Sanskrit word meaning "service," is a fundamental principle in Sanatan Dharma. It refers to the practice of selfless service for the welfare of others. Seva encourages us to lend a helping hand without expecting anything in return.

Understanding Seva

The word Seva comes from the Sanskrit root "sev," which means "to serve, to attend or wait upon, honor, or worship". The term Seva means "service, attendance, care". According to the notion of Sanatana-dharma, the eternal and intrinsic inclination of the living entity (atman) is to perform seva (service).

The Role of Seva in Daily Life

Seva plays a crucial role in our daily lives. It serves as a moral compass, guiding us to make choices that are good for both ourselves and our community. When we live by Seva, we create harmony and peace, but when we neglect it, it can lead to conflict and suffering.

Practical Application of Seva

To apply the concept of Seva in our daily life, we need to understand the consequences of our actions. Just as we saw with Moksha and Tapas, whether we're students, professionals, or citizens, we can always find ways to weave Seva into our lives.

Further Reading

If you're eager to delve deeper into the concept of Seva, here are some books I recommend:

1. "Seva: The Karma of Love" by Gurumayi Chidvilasananda.
2. "Seva: Sikh secrets on how to be good in the world" by Jasreen Mayal Khanna.
3. "Seva" by Leena Chawla Rajan.

These books will help you understand Seva more deeply and how you can make it a part of your daily life. They offer practical advice on how to live in accordance with Seva and achieve peace and fulfillment.

Ultimately, Seva, like the other core values of Sanatan Dharma, provides a framework for living a righteous and fulfilling life. By understanding and applying Seva in our daily life, we not only uplift others but also find true joy and purpose in our own lives.

Note:

Day 12

Satsang (सत्संग)

Satsang, a Sanskrit word meaning "association with truth," is a fundamental principle at the heart of Sanatan Dharma. It refers to the practice of associating with virtuous individuals and seeking the company of those on a similar spiritual journey. Satsang encourages us to surround ourselves with positive influences.

Understanding Satsang

The word Satsang comes from two Sanskrit words: "Sat", which means "truth", and "Sang", which means "association" or "company". Therefore, Satsang means "association with truth" or "being in the company of truth". It is a gathering of like-minded people who are united by a common goal - the quest for truth and the desire for spiritual growth.

The Role of Satsang in Daily Life

Satsang acts as a moral compass in our daily lives. It guides us to make decisions that are righteous and beneficial not only for ourselves but also for the society at large. When we practice

Satsang, it leads to harmony and peace in society. On the other hand, neglecting Satsang can lead to conflict and suffering.

Practical Application of Satsang

To apply the concept of Satsang in our daily lives, we need to understand the consequences of our actions. As students, our Satsang might be to study diligently and respect our teachers. As professionals, our Satsang might be to respect the time and effort of our colleagues and not take credit for their work. As citizens, our Satsang might be to respect the public property and not vandalize it.

Further Reading

If you're interested in diving deeper into Satsang, these books are a great place to start:

1. "The Heart of Yoga: Developing a Personal Practice" by T.K.V. Desikachar.
2. "Satsang with Mooji: Words That Point to Freedom" by Mooji.
3. "Satsang: In the Company of Truth" by Eckhart Tolle.

These books provide a comprehensive understanding of Satsang and its application in daily life. They offer practical advice on how to live in accordance with Satsang and achieve peace and fulfillment.

In essence, Satsang, a core value of Sanatan Dharma, provides a framework for living a righteous and meaningful life. By understanding and applying Satsang in our daily lives, we can contribute to the well-being of ourselves and society at large.

Note:

....
....
....
....
....
....

....
....
....

....
....
....
....

Day 13

Shraddha (श्रद्धा)

Shraddha, a Sanskrit word that translates to "faith," is a fundamental principle in Sanatan Dharma. It refers to the cultivation of faith, devotion, and trust in the divine. Shraddha encourages us to have faith in the divine and trust the process of life.

Understanding Shraddha

The word Shraddha comes from the Sanskrit root "shraddha," meaning "to have faith or trust". The term Shraddha means "faith, trust, confidence". According to the notion of Sanatana dharma, the eternal and intrinsic inclination of the living entity (atman) is to perform shraddha (faith).

The Role of Shraddha in Daily Life

Shraddha plays a crucial role in our daily lives. It helps us make righteous and beneficial decisions not only for ourselves but also for society at large. Upholding Shraddha leads to harmony and peace in society, while ignoring Shraddha can lead to conflict and hardship.

Practical Application of Shraddha

To apply the concept of Shraddha in our daily lives, we need to understand the consequences of our actions. As students, our Shraddha might be studying hard and respecting our teachers. As professionals, our Shraddha might be respecting the time and effort of our colleagues and not taking credit for their work. As citizens, our Shraddha might be respecting public property and not vandalizing it.

Further Reading

If you're curious to learn more about the concept of Shraddha, here are some books I recommend:

1. "Autobiography of a Yogi" by Paramahansa Yogananda.
2. "Shraddha - Andhashraddha" by Narendra Dabholkar.
3. "Shraddha" by R.K. Srikantakumaraswamy.

These books provide a comprehensive understanding of Shraddha and its application in daily life. They offer practical advice on how to live in accordance with Shraddha and achieve peace and fulfillment.

In essence, Shraddha is a guiding principle in Sanatan Dharma that can lead us towards a more meaningful and fulfilling life. By embracing and incorporating Shraddha into our everyday lives, we can make a positive impact on the world.

Note:

....
....
....
....
....
....

....
....
....

....
....
....
....

Day 14

Guru-Bhakti (गुरु-भक्ति)

Guru-Bhakti, a Sanskrit word meaning "devotion to the teacher," is a fundamental principle in Sanatan Dharma. It refers to the reverence and devotion towards the spiritual teacher. Guru-Bhakti encourages us to respect and learn from our spiritual guides.

Understanding Guru-Bhakti

The word Guru-Bhakti comes from two Sanskrit words: "Guru", which means "teacher", and "Bhakti", which means "devotion". Therefore, Guru-Bhakti means "devotion to the teacher". It's all about having deep respect and love for the Guru, who is seen as a guide towards spiritual enlightenment.

The Role of Guru-Bhakti in Daily Life

Guru-Bhakti plays a crucial role in our daily lives. It serves as a moral compass, guiding us to make decisions that are righteous and beneficial not only for ourselves but also for the society at large. Upholding Guru-Bhakti leads to harmony and peace in society, while neglecting Guru-Bhakti can lead to conflict and suffering.

Practical Application of Guru-Bhakti

To apply the concept of Guru-Bhakti in our daily lives, we need to understand the consequences of our actions. As students, our Guru-Bhakti might be to study diligently and respect our teachers. As professionals, our Guru-Bhakti might be about valuing your colleagues' work and not stealing credit. As citizens, our Guru-Bhakti might be to respect the public property and not vandalize it.

Further Reading

If you want to delve deeper into the concept of Guru-Bhakti, here are some books I recommend:

1. "Guruji: A Portrait of Sri K. Pattabhi Jois Through the Eyes of His Students" by Guy Donahaye and Eddie Stern.
2. "Guru-Bhakti Yoga" by Swami Sivananda.
3. "Guru: The Universal Teacher" by Swami Mukundananda.

These books provide a comprehensive understanding of Guru-Bhakti and its application in our daily lives. They offer practical advice on how to live in accordance with this principle and peace and fulfillment.

In essence, Guru-Bhakti, a core value of Sanatan Dharma, provides a framework for living a righteous and fulfilling life. By understanding and applying Guru-Bhakti in our daily lives, we can contribute to the well-being of ourselves and society at large.

Note:

Day 15

Vairagya (वैराग्य)

Vairagya, a Sanskrit word meaning "dispassion," is a fundamental principle in Sanatan Dharma. It's about learning to let go of our toward worldly desires and attachments. Vairagya encourages us to detach from materialistic desires.

Understanding Vairagya

The word Vairagya comes from the Sanskrit root "virag," which means "to become dispassionate". The term Vairagya means "dispassion, detachment". According to the notion of Sanatana-dharma, the eternal and intrinsic inclination of the living entity (atman) is to perform vairagya (dispassion).

The Role of Vairagya in Daily Life

Vairagya, or "dispassion," is like finding a sense of calm in a chaotic world. It's a guiding principle that helps us make good choices, not just for ourselves but also for the society at large. When we practice letting go of excessive desires, it creates a sense of peace and harmony in our communities. But if we cling too tightly to material things, it can lead to conflict and unhappiness.

Practical Application of Vairagya

To apply the concept of Vairagya in our daily lives, we need to understand the consequences of our actions. As students, our Vairagya might be to study diligently and respect our teachers. As professionals, our Vairagya might be to respect the time and effort of our colleagues and not take credit for their work. As citizens, our Vairagya might respect public property and not vandalize it.

Further Reading

If you'd like to explore Vairagya in more depth, here are some books I recommend:

1. "The Miracle of Mindfulness" by Thich Nhat Hanh.
2. "Vairagya Shatakam: of Bhartrihari" by Swami Madhavananda.
3. "How to Get Vairagya" by Swami Sivananda.

These books provide a comprehensive understanding of Vairagya and its application in daily life. They offer practical advice on how to live in accordance with Vairagya to find peace and fulfillment.

In essence, Vairagya, a core value of Sanatan Dharma, provides a framework for living a righteous and fulfilling life. By embracing and living by its principles in our daily lives, we can contribute to the well-being of ourselves and society at large.

Note:

Day 16

Tyaga (त्याग)

Tyaga, a Sanskrit word that translates to "renunciation," is a fundamental principle in Sanatan Dharma. It refers to the practice of renunciation and selflessness. Tyaga encourages us to let go of our selfish desires and work for the welfare of others.

Understanding Tyaga

The word Tyaga comes from the Sanskrit root "tyaj," which means "to abandon". The word Tyaga means "abandonment, relinquishment". According to the notion of Sanatana-dharma, the eternal and intrinsic inclination of the living entity (atman) is to perform tyaga (renunciation).

The Role of Tyaga in Daily Life

Tyaga, like Vairagya, acts as a moral compass in our lives. It helps us make choices that benefit everyone, not just ourselves but also for the society at large. Upholding Tyaga brings harmony and peace to society, while neglecting Tyaga can lead to conflict and suffering.

Practical Application of Tyaga

To apply the concept of Tyaga in our daily lives, we need to understand the consequences of our actions. As students, our Tyaga might be to study diligently and respect our teachers. As professionals, our Tyaga might be to respect the time and effort of our colleagues and not take credit for their work. As citizens, our Tyaga might respect public property and not vandalize it.

Further Reading

If you want to delve deeper into the concept of Tyaga, here are some books I recommended:

1. "The Bhagavad Gita" translated by Swami Sivananda.
2. "Tyag-patra" by Jainendra Kumar.
3. "Sannyasa and Tyaga" by Abbot George Burke (Swami Nirmalananda Giri).

These books provide a comprehensive understanding of Tyaga and practical ways to incorporate it into your everyday life. They offer practical advice on how to live selflessly and find inner peace and fulfillment.

In essence, Tyaga, a core value of Sanatan Dharma, provides a framework for living a righteous and fulfilling life. By understanding and applying Tyaga in our daily lives, we can contribute to the well-being of ourselves and those around us.

Note:

....
....
....

....
....
....
....
....
....

....
....
....
....

Day 17

Bhakti (भक्ति)

Bhakti, a Sanskrit word that translates to "devotion," is a fundamental principle in Sanatan Dharma. It refers to the cultivation of devotion and love towards the divine. Bhakti encourages us to love and devote ourselves to the divine.

Understanding Bhakti

The word Bhakti comes from the Sanskrit root "bhaj," which means "to share or partake". The word Bhakti means "devotion, participation". According to the notion of Sanatana-dharma, the eternal and intrinsic inclination of the living entity (atman) is to perform bhakti (devotion).

The Role of Bhakti in Daily Life

Bhakti plays a crucial role in our daily lives. It serves as a moral compass, guiding us to make decisions that are righteous and beneficial not only for ourselves but also for the society at large. Practicing Bhakti brings harmony and peace to society, while neglecting Bhakti can lead to conflict and suffering.

Practical Application of Bhakti

To apply the concept of Bhakti in our daily lives, we need to understand the consequences of our actions. As students, our Bhakti might be studying diligently and respecting our teachers. As professionals, our Bhakti might be respecting the time and effort of our colleagues and not taking credit for their work. As citizens, our Bhakti might be respecting public property and not vandalizing it.

Further Reading

If you're curious to explore Bhakti in more depth, here are some books I recommend:

1. "Bhakti Yoga: The Yoga of Love and Devotion" by Swami Vivekananda.
2. "The Nectar of Devotion: The Complete Science of Bhakti-Yoga" by A.C. Prabhupāda.
3. "Historical Development of the Bhakti Movement in India: Theory & Practice" by Professor Iwao Shima.

These books provide a comprehensive understanding of Bhakti and its application in our daily lives. They offer practical advice on how to live in accordance with Bhakti and achieve peace and fulfillment.

In essence, Bhakti, a core value of Sanatan Dharma, provides a framework for living a righteous and fulfilling life. By understanding and applying Bhakti in our daily lives, we can contribute to the well-being of ourselves and the world around us.

Note:

Day 18

Yajna (यज्ञ)

Yajna, a Sanskrit word that translates to "sacrifice," is a fundamental principle in Sanatan Dharma. It refers to the practice of performing selfless acts of sacrifice and offering. Yajna encourages us to give without expecting anything in return.

Understanding Yajna

The word Yajna comes from the Sanskrit root "yaj," which means "to worship, adore, honour, revere". The word Yajna means "worship, devotion to anything, prayer and praise, an act of worship or devotion, a form of offering or oblation, and sacrifice". According to the notion of Sanatana-dharma, the eternal and intrinsic inclination of the living entity (atman) is to perform yajna (sacrifice).

The Role of Yajna in Daily Life

Yajna plays an important role in our daily lives. It serves as a moral compass, guiding us to make decisions that are righteous and beneficial not only for ourselves but also for the society at large. When we embrace the spirit of Yajna, it leads us to harmony and peace in society. But if we only focus on ourselves and our own desires, neglecting Yajna can lead to conflict and suffering.

Practical Application of Yajna

To apply the concept of Yajna in our daily lives, we need to understand the consequences of our actions. As students, our Yajna might be to study diligently and respect our teachers. As professionals, our Yajna might be to respect the time and effort of our colleagues and not take credit for their work. As citizens, our Yajna might be to respect the public property, volunteer our time for community service, or donate to those in need.

Further Reading

If you're intrigued by the concept of Yajna and want to delve deeper into the concept of Yajna, here are some books I recommend:

1. "The Vedas: An Introduction to Hinduism's Sacred Texts" by Roshen Dalal.
2. "Yajna: A Comprehensive Survey" by Swami Jitatmananda.
3. "Yajna: A Scientific Perspective" by Prakash Pandey.

These books provide a comprehensive understanding of Yajna and its application in our daily lives. They offer practical advice on how to live in accordance with Yajna and find peace and fulfillment.

In essence, Yajna, as a core value of Sanatan Dharma, provides a framework for living a righteous and fulfilling life. By embracing the spirit of Yajna and applying it in our daily lives, we can contribute to the well-being of ourselves and society at large.

Note:

....
....
....
....
....
....

....
....
....

....
....
....
....

Day 19

Dhyana (ध्यान)

Dhyana, a Sanskrit word that translates to "meditation," is a fundamental principle in Sanatan Dharma. It refers to the practice of meditation and mindfulness. Dhyana encourages us to be present in the moment and be aware of our thoughts and actions.

Understanding Dhyana

The word Dhyana comes from the Sanskrit root "dhyai," which means "to think of". The word Dhyana means "meditation, contemplation". According to the notion of Sanatana-dharma, the eternal and intrinsic inclination of the living entity (atman) is to perform dhyana (meditation).

The Role of Dhyana in Daily Life

Dhyana plays a crucial role in our daily lives. It helps us become more aware of our thoughts and actions, guiding us towards good choices that benefit not just ourselves but everyone around us. Upholding Dhyana leads to harmony and peace in our society. However, if we ignore this inner reflection, such as neglecting Dhyana, it can lead to conflict and suffering.

Practical Application of Dhyana

To apply the concept of Dhyana in our daily lives, we need to understand the consequences of our actions. As students, our Dhyana might be to study diligently and respect our teachers. As professionals, our Dhyana might be to respect the time and effort of our colleagues and not take credit for their work. As citizens, our Dhyana might be to respect the public property and not vandalize it.

Further Reading

If you want to delve deeper into the concept of Dhyana, here are some books I recommend:

1. "The Yoga Sutras of Patanjali" translated by Swami Satchidananda.
2. "Dhyana Yoga" by Swami Sivananda.
3. "OSHO Dhyan Yog" by OSHO.

These books provide a comprehensive understanding of Dhyana and its application in our daily lives. They offer practical advice on how to live in accordance with Dhyana and achieve peace and fulfillment.

In essence, Dhyana, a core value of Sanatan Dharma, provides a framework for living a righteous and fulfilling life. By understanding and applying Dhyana in our daily lives, we can contribute to the well-being of ourselves and the society at large.

Note:

....
....
....
....
....
....

....
....
....
....
....
....

....
....

Day 20

Pranayama (प्राणायाम)

Pranayama, a Sanskrit word that translates to "breath control," is a fundamental principle in Sanatan Dharma. It refers to the practice of regulating the breath to control the prana (life force). Pranayama encourages us to control our breath and attain peace and calmness.

Understanding Pranayama

The word Pranayama comes from two Sanskrit words: "Prana", which means "life force", and "Ayama", which means "control" or "regulation". Therefore, Pranayama means "control of the life force". It is a method of controlling and regulating breath to control the life force or energy within us.

The Role of Pranayama in Daily Life

Pranayama plays a powerful role in our daily lives. It serves as a tool for achieving physical health, mental clarity, and spiritual growth. Regular practice of Pranayama can help reduce stress, improve concentration, and promote overall well-being.

Practical Application of Pranayama

To apply the concept of Pranayama in our daily lives, we need to understand the techniques and benefits of different types of Pranayama. Some of the common types of Pranayama include Anulom Vilom, Bhramari, and Kapalabhati. Regular practice of these techniques can help optimize oxygen intake, enhance lung capacity, stimulate the parasympathetic nervous system, induce a state of relaxation, and reduce stress.

Further Reading

If you want to delve deeper into the concept of Pranayama, here are some books I recommend:

1. "Light on Pranayama" by B.K.S. Iyengar.
2. "Prana and Pranayama" by Swami Nirjananda Saraswat.
3. "The Science of Pranayama" by Swami Sivananda.

These books provide a comprehensive understanding of Pranayama and its application in daily life. They offer practical advice on how to practice Pranayama and achieve peace and fulfillment.

In essence, Pranayama, a core value of Sanatan Dharma, provides a framework for living a healthy and fulfilling life. By understanding and practicing Pranayama in our daily lives, we can contribute to the well-being of ourselves and society at large.

Note:

....
....
....
....
....
....

....
....
....

....
....
....
....

Day 21

Niyama (नियम)

Niyama, a Sanskrit word meaning "observance," is a fundamental principle in Sanatan Dharma. It refers to the practice of observing personal disciplines for self-purification. Niyama encourages us to follow certain disciplines to purify our body and mind.

Understanding Niyama

The word Niyama comes from the Sanskrit root "niyam" which means "to bind or restrain". The word Niyama means "observance, rule, law". According to the notion of Sanatana-dharma, the eternal and intrinsic inclination of the living entity (atman) is to perform niyama (observance).

The Role of Niyama in Daily Life

Niyama serves as a moral compass, guiding us to make decisions that are righteous and beneficial not only for ourselves but also for the society at large. Upholding Niyama fosters harmony and peace in our society, while neglecting Niyama can lead to conflict and suffering.

Practical Application of Niyama

To apply the concept of Niyama in our daily lives, we need to understand the consequences of our actions. As students, our Niyama might be to study with dedication and respect our teachers. As professionals, our Niyama might be to respect the time and effort of our colleagues and not take credit for their work. As citizens, our Niyama might be to respect public property and not vandalize it.

Further Reading

If you're interested in delving deeper into the concept of Niyama, here are some books I recommend:

1. "The Heart of Yoga: Developing a Personal Practice" by T.K.V. Desikachar.
2. "The Yamas & Niyamas: Exploring Yoga's Ethical Practice" by Deborah Adele.
3. "Inside the Yoga Sutras: A Comprehensive Sourcebook for the Study & Practice of Patanjali's Yoga Sutras" by Reverend Jaganath Carrera.

These books provide a comprehensive understanding of Niyama and its application in daily life. They offer practical advice on how to practice Niyama and achieve peace and fulfillment.

In essence, Niyama, a core value of Sanatan Dharma, provides a framework for living a righteous and fulfilling life. By understanding and practicing Niyama daily, we can nurture our inner selves and the society at large.

Note:

Day 22

Sama (सम)

Sama, a Sanskrit word that translates to "equanimity," is a fundamental principle in Sanatan Dharma. It refers to the practice of cultivating equanimity and mental balance. Sama encourages us to maintain a balanced state of mind in all situations.

Understanding Sama

The word Sama comes from the Sanskrit root "sam" which means "to calm or pacify". The term Sama means "calmness, tranquility". According to the notion of Sanatana-dharma, the eternal and intrinsic inclination of the living entity (atman) is to perform sama (calmness).

The Role of Sama in Daily Life

Sama plays a crucial role in our daily lives. It serves as a moral compass, guiding us to make decisions that are righteous and beneficial not only for ourselves but also for the society at large. When we practice Sama, it leads to harmony and peace in society, but if we let ourselves get carried away by emotions, as in neglect Sama, it can lead to conflict and suffering.

Practical Application of Sama

To apply the concept of Sama in our daily lives, we need to understand the consequences of our actions. As students, our Sama might be to study diligently and respect our teachers. As professionals, our Sama might be to respect the time and effort of our colleagues and not take credit for their work. As citizens, our Sama might be to respect public property and not vandalize it.

Further Reading

If you want to delve deeper into the concept of Sama, here are some books I recommend:

1. "The Bhagavad Gita" translated by Swami Sivananda.
2. "The Science of Being and Art of Living" by Maharishi Mahesh Yogi.
3. "The Power of Now: A Guide to Spiritual Enlightenment" by Eckhart Tolle.
4. "Mindfulness in Plain English" by Bhante Henepola Gunaratana.

These books provide a comprehensive understanding of Sama and practical guidance on cultivating inner peace and equanimity in daily life. They offer practical advice on how to practice Sama and achieve peace and fulfillment, even in the face of adversity.

In essence, Sama, a core value of Sanatan Dharma, provides a framework for living a righteous and fulfilling life. By understanding and practicing Sama in our daily life, we can contribute to the well-being of ourselves and the society at large.

Note:

....
....
....
....
....
....

....
....
....
....
....
....

....
....
....
....

Day 23

Dana (दान)

Dana, a Sanskrit word meaning "generosity," is a fundamental principle in Sanatan Dharma. It refers to the practice of generosity and charity towards others. Dana encourages us to be generous and help others.

Understanding Dana

The word Dana comes from the Sanskrit root "da," which means "to give". The term Dana means "giving, gift, donation". According to the notion of Sanatana-dharma, the eternal and intrinsic inclination of the living entity (atman) is to perform dana (generosity) without expecting anything in return.

The Role of Dana in Daily Life

Dana plays a crucial role in our daily lives. It serves as a moral compass, guiding us to make decisions that are righteous and beneficial not only for ourselves but also for the society at large. Upholding Dana leads to harmony and peace in society, while neglecting Dana can lead to conflict and suffering.

Practical Application of Dana

To embrace the concept of Dana in our daily lives, we need to understand the consequences of our actions. As students, our Dana might be to study diligently and respect our teachers. As professionals, our Dana might be to respect the time and effort of our colleagues and not take credit for their work. As citizens, our Dana might be to respect the public property and not vandalize it.

Further Reading

If you want to delve deeper into the concept of Dana, here are some books I recommend:

1. "The Bhagavad Gita" translated by Swami Sivananda.
2. "The Power of Unwavering Focus" by Dandapani.
3. "Dana: Reciprocity and Patronage in Buddhism" by Anand Singh.

These books provide a comprehensive understanding of Dana and its application in daily life. They offer practical advice on how to practice Dana and achieve peace and fulfillment.

In essence, Dana, a core value of Sanatan Dharma, provides a framework for living a righteous and fulfilling life. By embracing generosity and sharing our blessings with others, we not only uplift those around us but also find deeper meaning and fulfillment in our own lives.

As we continue through the remaining Days, we'll explore even more values and concepts that are at the heart of Sanatan Dharma—providing a comprehensive understanding of this ancient philosophy. This book is a journey of self-discovery and spiritual growth, and I hope it serves as a valuable guide for all of you, dear readers.

Note:

....
....
....

....
....
....
....
....
....

....
....
....
....

Day 24

Shanti (शांति)

Shanti, a Sanskrit word meaning "peace," is a fundamental principle in Sanatan Dharma. It refers to the practice of cultivating inner peace and tranquility. Shanti encourages us to find peace within ourselves and spread it to others.

Understanding Shanti

The word Shanti comes from the Sanskrit root "sham," which means "to calm or pacify". The word Shanti means "peace, tranquility". According to the notion of Sanatana-dharma, the eternal and intrinsic inclination of the living entity (atman) is to perform shanti (peace).

The Role of Shanti in Daily Life

Shanti plays a crucial role in our daily lives. It serves as our guiding principle, helping us to make decisions that are righteous and beneficial not only for ourselves but also for society at large. Upholding Shanti leads to harmony and peace in society, while neglecting Shanti can lead to conflict and suffering.

Practical Application of Shanti

To apply the concept of Shanti in our daily lives, we need to understand the consequences of our actions. As students, our Shanti might be to study diligently and respect our teachers. As professionals, our Shanti might involve maintaining a peaceful work environment and appreciating the efforts of colleagues. As citizens, our Shanti might be to respect public property and not vandalize it.

Further Reading

If you're intrigued by the concept of Shanti, here are some books I recommend:

1. "Peace Is Every Step: The Path of Mindfulness in Everyday Life" by Thich Nhat Hanh.
2. "The Power of Now: A Guide to Spiritual Enlightenment" by Eckhart Tolle.
3. "Wherever You Go, There You Are: Mindfulness Meditation in Everyday Life" by Jon Kabat-Zinn.
4. "The Miracle of Mindfulness: An Introduction to the Practice of Meditation" by Thich Nhat Hanh.

These books provide a comprehensive understanding of Shanti and its application in our daily lives. They offer practical advice on how to practice Shanti and achieve peace and fulfillment.

In essence, Shanti, a core value of Sanatan Dharma, provides a framework for living a righteous and fulfilling life. By understanding and practicing Shanti in our daily life, we can contribute to the well-being of ourselves and the society at large.

Note:

....
....
....
....
....
....

....
....
....

....
....
....
....

Day 25

Viveka (विवेक)

Viveka, a Sanskrit word that translates to "discernment," is a fundamental principle in Sanatan Dharma. It refers to the practice of discernment and discrimination between the real and the unreal. Viveka encourages us to distinguish between the eternal truth and the transient world.

Understanding Viveka

The word Viveka comes from the Sanskrit root "vich" which means "to sift, separate, deprive, discriminate, discern, or judge". The word Viveka means "discrimination, judgement, discernment, discretion, consideration, discussion, investigation, distinction, difference, true knowledge, a receptacle for water, basin, reservoir, reflection, right judgement, and a water trough". According to the notion of Sanatana-dharma, the eternal and intrinsic inclination of the living entity (atman) is to perform viveka (discernment).

The Role of Viveka in Daily Life

Viveka acts as your moral compass, steering you towards actions that benefit not only yourself but also society at large. When we embrace discernment, it fosters harmony and peace in our communities. But if we ignore this inner wisdom, it can lead to disagreements and sufferings.

Practical Application of Viveka

To apply the concept of Viveka in our daily lives, we need to understand the consequences of our actions. As students, our Viveka might be to study diligently and respect our teachers. As professionals, our Viveka might be to respect the time and effort of our colleagues and not take credit for their work. As citizens, our Viveka might be to respect public property and not vandalize it.

Further Reading

If you want to delve deeper into the concept of Viveka, here are some books I recommend:

1. "Vivekachudamani" by Adi Shankaracharya.
2. "The Bhagavad Gita" translated by Swami Sivananda.
3. "The Power of Unwavering Focus" by Dandapani.
4. "Complete Works of Swami Vivekananda (9 vols.)" by Swami Vivekananda.

These books provide a comprehensive understanding of Viveka and its application in daily life. They offer practical advice on how to practice Viveka and make choices that lead to peace and fulfillment.

In essence, Viveka, a core value of Sanatan Dharma, provides a framework for living a righteous and fulfilling life. By understanding and practicing Viveka in our daily lives, we can contribute to the well-being of ourselves and the society at large.

Note:

....
....
....
....

....
....
....
....

....
....
....
....

Day 26

Svadhyaya (स्वाध्याय)

Svadhyaya, a Sanskrit word that translates to "self-study," is a fundamental principle in Sanatan Dharma. It refers to the practice of self-study and reflection on sacred texts. Svadhyaya encourages us to introspect and learn from the wisdom of the scriptures.

Understanding Svadhyaya

The word Svadhyaya comes from the Sanskrit roots "sva," meaning "own, one's own, self, the human soul," and "adhyaya," meaning "a lesson, lecture, or reading". Therefore, Svadhyaya literally means "one's own reading, lesson" or "to learn the lessons of your own soul". According to the notion of Sanatana-dharma, the eternal and intrinsic inclination of the living entity (atman) is to perform Svadhyaya (self-study).

The Role of Svadhyaya in Daily Life

Svadhyaya, like the other principles, acts as a moral compass in our lives. It helps us make good choices that are righteous and beneficial not only for ourselves but also for the society at large.

Upholding Svadhyaya leads to harmony and peace in society, while neglecting Svadhyaya can lead to conflict and suffering.

Practical Application of Svadhyaya

To apply the concept of Svadhyaya in our daily lives, we need to understand the consequences of our actions. As students, our Svadhyaya might be to study diligently and respect our teachers. As professionals, our Svadhyaya might be to respect the time and effort of our colleagues and not take credit for their work. As citizens, our Svadhyaya might be to respect public property and not vandalize it.

Further Reading

If you want to delve deeper into the concept of Svadhyaya, here are some books I recommend:

1. "The Bhagavad Gita" translated by Swami Sivananda.
2. "The Power of Unwavering Focus" by Dandapani.
3. "Vivekachudamani" by Adi Shankaracharya.
4. "Complete Works of Swami Vivekananda (9 vols.)" by Swami Vivekananda.

These books provide a comprehensive understanding of Svadhyaya and its application in daily life. They offer practical advice on practicing Svadhyaya and achieving peace and fulfillment.

In essence, Svadhyaya, a core value of Sanatan Dharma, provides a framework for living a righteous and fulfilling life. By understanding and practicing Svadhyaya in our daily lives, we can contribute to the well-being of ourselves and the society at large.

Note:

....
....
....
....
....
....

....
....
....
....
....
....

....
....
....
....

Day 27

Sankirtan (संकीर्तन)

Sankirtan, a Sanskrit word meaning "group chanting," is a fundamental principle in Sanatan Dharma. It refers to the practice of group chanting or singing of divine names and hymns. Sankirtan encourages us to participate in collective spiritual activities that uplift our spirits.

Understanding Sankirtan

The word Sankirtan comes from the Sanskrit roots "sam," meaning "complete", and "kirtan", which means "praising," "celebrating" or "glorifying". Therefore, Sankirtan literally means "complete glorification" or "complete celebration". According to the notion of Sanatana-dharma, the eternal and intrinsic inclination of the living entity (atman) is to perform Sankirtan.

The Role of Sankirtan in Daily Life

Sankirtan plays a crucial role in our daily lives. It serves as a moral compass, guiding us to make decisions that are righteous and beneficial not only for ourselves but also for the society at large. Upholding Sankirtan leads to harmony and peace in society, while neglecting Sankirtan can lead to conflict and suffering.

Practical Application of Sankirtan

To apply the concept of Sankirtan in our daily lives, we need to understand the consequences of our actions. As students, our Sankirtan might be to study diligently and respect our teachers. As professionals, our Sankirtan might be to respect the time and effort of our colleagues and not take credit for their work. As citizens, our Sankirtan might be to respect public property and not vandalize it.

Further Reading

If you want to delve deeper into the concept of Sankirtan, here are some books I recommend:

1. "Japa Yoga: A Comprehensive Treatise on Mantra Sastra" by Swami Sivananda.
2. "Chanting Krishna: The Mantra Meditation and the Science of Sound" by Lokanath Swami.
3. "Mantra Yoga and Primal Sound: Secret of Seed (Bija) Mantras" by David Frawley.
4. "Chant and Be Happy: The Power of Mantra Meditation" by A. C. Bhaktivedanta Swami Prabhupada.

These books provide a comprehensive understanding of Sankirtan and its application in daily life. They offer practical advice on practicing Sankirtan and finding peace and fulfillment.

In essence, Sankirtan, a core value of Sanatan Dharma, provides a framework for living a righteous and fulfilling life. By understanding and practicing Sankirtan in our daily lives, we can contribute to the well-being of ourselves and the society at large.

Note:

....
....
....

....
....
....
....
....
....

....
....
....
....

Day 28

Samadhi (समाधि)

Samadhi, a Sanskrit word that translates to "deep meditation," is a fundamental principle in Sanatan Dharma. It refers to the state of deep meditation and spiritual absorption. Samadhi is the ultimate goal of many spiritual practices where the practitioner experiences oneness with the divine.

Understanding Samadhi

The word Samadhi comes from the Sanskrit root "sam-a-dha," which means "to collect or bring together". Therefore, Samadhi literally means "bringing together" or "concentration". According to the notion of Sanatana-dharma, the eternal and intrinsic inclination of the living entity (atman) is to perform samadhi (deep meditation).

The Role of Samadhi in Daily Life

Samadhi plays an important role in our daily lives. It's like a guiding star, illuminating the path toward making decisions that are righteous and beneficial not only for ourselves but also for society at large. Upholding Samadhi leads to harmony and peace in society, while neglecting Samadhi can lead to conflict and suffering.

Practical Application of Samadhi

To apply the concept of Samadhi in our daily lives, we need to understand the consequences of our actions. As students, our Samadhi might be to study sincerely and respect our teachers. As professionals, our Samadhi might be to respect the time and effort of our colleagues and not take credit for their work. As citizens, our Samadhi might be to respect the public property and not vandalize it.

Further Reading

If you're curious to delve deeper into the concept of Samadhi, here are some books I recommend:

1. "Autobiography of a Yogi" by Paramahansa Yogananda.
2. "The Experience of Samadhi: An In-depth Exploration of Buddhist Meditation" by Richard Shankman.
3. "Samadhi: The Highest State Of Wisdom: Yoga the Sacred Science" by Swami Rama.
4. "Path of Serenity and Insight: An Explanation of the Buddhist Jhanas" by Henepola Gunaratana.

These books provide a comprehensive understanding of Samadhi and its application in daily life. They offer practical advice on how incorporate Samadhi into your daily life and find peace and fulfillment.

In essence, Samadhi, a core value of Sanatan Dharma, provides a framework for living a righteous and fulfilling life. By understanding and practicing Samadhi in our daily lives, we can tap into our inner potential and live a more meaningful and fulfilling life.

Note:

....
....
....

....
....
....
....
....
....

....
....
....
....

Day 29

Ananda (आनंद)

Ananda, a Sanskrit term that translates to "bliss," is a fundamental principle in Sanatan Dharma. It refers to the experience of bliss and joy through spiritual realization. It's the kind of joy that doesn't depend on external things like possessions or achievements. Ananda encourages us to seek happiness not in material possessions but in spiritual growth.

Understanding Ananda

The word Ananda comes from the Sanskrit root "nand," which means "to rejoice or be glad". Therefore, Ananda literally means "bliss, happiness, joy, delight, pleasure, or enjoyment". According to the notion of Sanatana-dharma, the eternal and intrinsic inclination of the living entity (atman) is to perform ananda (bliss).

The Role of Ananda in Daily Life

Ananda acts as a guiding light, showing us that true happiness lies in our inner world, not in material possessions. It helps us to make decisions that are righteous and beneficial not only for ourselves but also for the society at large. Upholding Ananda leads to harmony and peace in society, while neglecting Ananda can lead to conflict and suffering.

Practical Application of Ananda

Think of Ananda as a way to find joy in the simple things. To apply the concept of Ananda in our daily lives, we need to first understand the consequences of our actions. As students, our Ananda might mean finding joy in learning and appreciating the guidance of our teachers. As professionals, our Ananda might be respecting the time and effort of our colleagues and not taking credit for their work. As citizens, our Ananda might be respecting public property and not vandalizing it.

Further Reading

If you'd like to learn more about the concept of Ananda, here are some recommended books:

1. "The Art of Happiness" by Dalai Lama and Howard Cutler.
2. "The Power of Now: A Guide to Spiritual Enlightenment" by Eckhart Tolle.
3. "Wherever You Go, There You Are: Mindfulness Meditation in Everyday Life" by Jon Kabat-Zinn.
4. "The Miracle of Mindfulness: An Introduction to the Practice of Meditation" by Thich Nhat Hanh.

These books provide a comprehensive understanding of Ananda and its application in daily life. They offer practical advice on how to practice Ananda and achieve peace and fulfillment.

In essence, Ananda, a core value of Sanatan Dharma, provides a framework for living a righteous and fulfilling life. By understanding and practicing Ananda in our daily lives, we can experience true fulfillment and contribute to the well-being of ourselves and society at large.

Note:

....
....
....
....
....
....

....
....
....

....
....
....
....

Day 30

Paramarth (परमार्थ)

Paramarth, a Sanskrit word meaning "ultimate truth," is a fundamental principle in Sanatan Dharma. It's about seeking the ultimate truth and realizing the divine. Paramarth encourages us to strive for the highest truth beyond the physical and mental realms.

Understanding Paramarth

The word Paramarth comes from the Sanskrit root "parama-artha", which means "ultimate purpose". Therefore, Paramarth literally means "ultimate truth or purpose". According to the notion of Sanatana-dharma, the eternal and intrinsic inclination of the living entity (atman) is to perform paramarth (ultimate truth).

The Role of Paramarth in Daily Life

Paramarth plays an important role in our daily lives. It serves as a moral compass, guiding us to make decisions that are righteous and beneficial not only for ourselves but also for the society at large. When we live by Paramarth, it leads to harmony and peace in society, while neglecting Paramarth can lead to conflict and suffering.

Practical Application of Paramarth

To apply the concept of Paramarth in our daily lives, we need to understand the consequences of our actions. As students, our Paramarth might be to study diligently and respect our teachers. As professionals, our Paramarth might be to value your colleagues' time and effort and not take credit for their work. As citizens, our Paramarth might be to respect public property and not vandalize it.

Further Reading

If you want to delve deeper into the concept of Paramarth, here are some books I recommend:

1. "Autobiography of a Yogi" by Paramahansa Yogananda.
2. "Paramarth Prasang" by Swami Virajananda.
3. "Books by Swami Paramarthananda" by Arsha Avinash Foundation.
4. "The Power of Now: A Guide to Spiritual Enlightenment" by Eckhart Tolle.

These books provide a comprehensive understanding of Paramarth and its application in daily life.

In essence, Paramarth, a core value of Sanatan Dharma, provides a framework for living a righteous and meaningful life. By embracing and practicing Paramarth in our daily lives, we not only improve our own lives but also make the world a better place.

Note:

....
....
....

....
....
....
....
....
....

....
....
....
....

Day 31

The Journey of Sanatan Dharma

Sanatan Dharma, often referred to as the eternal way of life, provides a set of universal principles that guide individuals towards a fulfilling and harmonious life. When these principles are not followed, it can lead to a life of confusion, dissatisfaction, and conflict.

For instance, consider a person who neglects the principle of **Ahimsa** (non-violence). They may engage in harmful actions towards others, leading to personal guilt, social isolation, and potential legal consequences. Similarly, a person who frequently lies, neglecting the principle of truthfulness (**Satya**), might find their relationships crumbling due to broken trust.

But when we embrace these principles, it can lead to profound benefits. For example, a person practicing **Sama** (equanimity) might find themselves more resilient in the face of life's ups and downs, leading to a more peaceful and content life. Similarly, someone who practices **Dana** (generosity) might discover that giving not only brings joy to others but also enriches their own life.

Starting the journey of adopting Sanatan Dharma in daily life can doesn't require drastic changes. Start with small steps. One could start by practicing **Ahimsa** by being kind to others, or **Satya** by being honest in their interactions. Regular meditation and self-reflection can help cultivate **Sama** and **Dhyana** (meditation), while acts of charity can promote **Dana**.

Let's bring more awareness with some imaginary examples:

1. **Raj** was often dishonest in his dealings, which led to a loss of trust among his friends and colleagues and left him isolated. After adopting the principle of **Satya**, he noticed a significant improvement in his relationships.

2. **Anita** was always stressed about her work. After learning about **Sama**, she started practicing equanimity and found herself more at peace, even in stressful situations.

3. **Vikram** was known for his short temper. After understanding the principle of **Ahimsa**, he made a conscious effort to control his anger, which improved his interpersonal relationships.

4. **Meena** always chased after material possessions. After she started practicing **Ananda**, she found joy in spiritual growth rather than materialistic pursuits.

5. **Ravi** was a successful businessman but felt something was missing in his life. After adopting the principle of **Dana**, he started a charity and found meaning and purpose in helping others.

The principles of Sanatan Dharma serve as a compass guiding us toward a life of purpose, meaning, and harmony. Ignoring these principles can lead to negative consequences, while embracing them can lead to personal growth and societal harmony. The journey of adopting these principles is a personal one, filled with learning and self-discovery.

It's a journey towards understanding the ultimate truth - the essence of Sanatan Dharma.

In the quest for spiritual growth, many individuals embark on pilgrimages, immersing themselves in the euphoria of hymns and dances, hoping for a touch of the divine. You find yourself caught up in the excitement of singing, dancing, and feeling a glimpse of something extraordinary. But is this fleeting feeling of wonder a true spiritual awakening? Or is it more like mistaking a firefly's glow for the brilliance of a shooting star?

Sometimes, we get so swept up in the moment that we forget true transformation requires more than just temporary excitement. It's easy to get lost in the dreamlike state of a spiritual high, forgetting about the practical realities of life. These enchanting experiences can be wonderful, but they don't always equal deep personal growth.

Authentic and enduring transformation requires diligent effort and attention to various facets of life – intellectual growth (IQ), emotional understanding (EQ), and spiritual connection (SQ). It's not solely about the harmonious melodies of bhajans or the rhythmic movements of dance; it's about fostering a balanced and conscious life.

Implementing the values of Sanatan Dharma can effectively nurture these areas. The principles of Sanatan Dharma guide us towards intellectual clarity, emotional stability, and spiritual enlightenment, thereby enhancing our IQ, EQ, and SQ, respectively.

So, the next time you have a magical spiritual experience, remember that it's just one step on a longer journey. True transformation comes from continuously working on your mind, heart, and spirit. It's through this comprehensive effort that the authentic magic of transformation unfolds. By adhering to the principles of Sanatan Dharma, you embark on a journey towards achieving growth in all aspects of life.

Endnote

Over a transformative 30-day journey, we immersed ourselves in the profound teachings of Sanatan Dharma. This book emerges as a guiding light, offering fresh perspectives with each read. It's designed to be a daily source of reflection, revealing insights and values that can revolutionize your life. Every chapter is a step toward deeper wisdom, inspiring you to integrate these teachings into your daily actions.

Consider this book a key component of your personal growth, encouraging you to embrace its wisdom fully. As you engage with each chapter, you'll be motivated to learn and live more meaningfully. My aim was to demystify the universal values of Sanatan Dharma, showing how they can enhance your life.

But the exploration doesn't end here. I urge you to adopt these values actively, creating strategies to weave them into the fabric of your life. This book isn't just a passive read; it's a dynamic tool for ongoing transformation, urging you to live in sync with the ageless wisdom of Sanatan Dharma.

The secrets of the universe may seem complex, but with the right approach, they become much easier to understand. This book aims to simplify these secrets and make them accessible to you. As you journey through these pages, you, too, will gain insights into these profound truths.

Remember, the pursuit of knowledge is a continuous process. Each day presents a new opportunity to enrich your life with these timeless teachings. Written in simple English, this book is designed to be accessible to readers in India and around the world.

So, enjoy the journey! May the wisdom of Sanatan Dharma fill your life with joy, meaning, and a deeper understanding of the world around you.

About the Author

Shantilal Patel

Greetings! You can call me Shantilalbhai—I'm affectionately known by that name among friends. My professional journey began like many of yours, working for others. Armed with a degree in electronics engineering and a part-time MBA, I honed my skills as a production manager in an electronics manufacturing company from 1989 to 1991.

However, an insatiable desire for something more drove me. In 1992, that aspiration materialized when I founded Nishan Power Converters. The motivation? The frustration caused by frequent power cuts disrupting our lives. I knew there had to be a better solution.

And so, Nishan was born—a venture dedicated to providing reliable backup power solutions. We started by creating inverters and UPS systems for homes and businesses, empowering everyone to combat those pesky blackouts. But Nishan isn't merely about products; it embodies a core value: **"to leave a mark of safety and comfort by applying innovative ideas that enhance people's lives."** This principle fuels us daily.

At Nishan, the customer reigns supreme. Whether you seek guidance on choosing the right product or have questions about your existing system, we're here for you. Yet, my quest for knowledge extends beyond business. I'm a lifelong learner, constantly seeking personal growth.

Over the years, I've delved into practices like the Silva mind control method, Pranic healing, and workshops on fasting and self-discovery. As a certified NLP (Neuro-Linguistic Programming) practitioner, trained by some of the best in the field, I'm also a proud founding member of the BNI chapter in Bhiwandi.

Throughout this journey, my foundation remains rooted in Sanatan Dharma values. These 30 powerful principles guide us through life's toughest challenges. So, as you turn the pages of this book, remember—it's not just the work of a businessman. It's a message from a fellow Bhartiya, a lifelong learner, and someone deeply committed to making a positive impact on the world.

Let's embark on this transformative journey together!